PRAYERS FOR
inclusion
and diversity

Rupert Bristow

Augsburg Books
MINNEAPOLIS

*For Sarah and for The Folkestone Rainbow Centre,
which is living out many of the themes in this book.*

PRAYERS FOR INCLUSION AND DIVERSITY

© Copyright 2012 Rupert Bristow.
Original edition published in English under the title PRAYERS FOR INCLUSION AND DIVERSITY by Kevin Mayhew Ltd, Buxhall, England.

This edition published in 2020 by Fortress Press. All rights reserved. Except for brief quotations in critical articles or reviwes, no part of this book may be reproduced in any manner without prior written permission from the publisher. Email copyright@augsburgfortress.org or write to Permissions, Fortress Press, PO Box 1209, Minneapolis, MN 55440-1209.

Cover image: © iStock 2020: Broken tiles mosaic seamless pattern by phokin
Cover design: Emily Drake

Print ISBN: 978-1-5064-6016-1

Contents

About the author	5
Foreword	7
Introduction	9

Inclusion

Giving and receiving	12
Variety in the world	14
Freedom and democracy	16
Faith and faiths	18
Personal and collective	20
Communicating and obeying	22
Roles in family and society	24
Competing and collaborating	28
Humanity, flora and fauna	30
Nature and nurture	32
The imprisoned and oppressed	34
The righteous and the sinner	36
The bully and the bullied	40
Atheists and agnostics	42
Leadership and discipleship	44
Growing old	46
Mental health	48
Racism	50
Redundancy and unemployment	52
Youth culture	54
Worry	56
Innovators/completer finishers	58
Hot and cold	60
Solitude and gregariousness	62
Music and musicians	64
Animals and pets	66
Rural and urban	68
Sport and leisure	70
Reading and writing	72
Communities and networks	74

Diversity

Ethnicity	78
Religion	80
Gender	82
Sexuality	84
Disability	86
Height and weight	88
Age	90
Wealth and poverty	92
Beauty and utility	94
Spiritual and physical	96
The unborn	98
The dead	100
Planning and spontaneity	102
The healthy and the sick	104
Despair and hope	106
Abuse	108
Alcohol addiction	110
Cancer	112
Coping with suffering	114
Crime	116
Dealing with difficult people	118
Debt	120
Dementia	122
Divorce	124
Domestic violence	126
Drugs	128
Family breakdown	130
Gambling	132
Politics	134
War and peace	136

About the author

Rupert Bristow was Director of Education for Canterbury Diocese and a governor of Canterbury Christ Church University from 1995 until his retirement in 2008 and is active as a Reader in Trinity Benefice, Folkestone. He graduated from London University as an external student at Cambridgeshire College of Arts and Technology, has taught on VSO (in Rwanda), was the second Director of the UK Council for Overseas Student Affairs (UKCOSA), and then Dean of Student Services at London South Bank University. He has also been a special adviser to a House of Commons select committee, edited and written for various educational publications and chaired Kent SACRE (Standing Advisory Council for Religious Education). He is an Honorary Fellow of Canterbury Christ Church University.

Other books by Rupert Bristow

Prayers for Education (2005)
Only Connect (2009)
Sunday Intercessions (2010)
Prayers for Parishes (2011)

Foreword

Rupert spent decades fighting for the welfare of overseas students as Director of the United Kingdom Council for Overseas Student Affairs (UKCOSA). It was his passionate message that overseas students are part of that 'one humanity' and 'one world' to which we belong, and therefore must be treated as well as everybody else, that first drew my attention. He repeatedly urged government ministers and officials, and the college and university authorities, to treat these students as Britain's future ambassadors to the various foreign countries and their homeland to which they would return after their studies. This was music to my ears as the Chaplain to Ghanaian students and immigrants to the UK. It was radical, as it was electric, firing the imagination of many like me working among overseas students who believe that these students with their diverse cultures bring richness to British life.

Rupert and I have been engaged in relentless prayer for the unity and peace of the world, and in intense theological discussions on the nature of Christian prayer. His firmly-held Christian beliefs in creation, incarnation and reconciliation through Christ inform and inspire all his works, especially *Prayers for Inclusion and Diversity*. It is therefore important for me in highly recommending this book of prayers for use in churches and in personal devotion to highlight briefly the biblical and evangelical context in which these prayers will receive the blessing of the Lord for the glory of God and the salvation of humankind:

Firstly, the effectiveness and the power of these prayers do not lie in the clever words or the wisdom of its author, but in whether the lives of users of this prayer book are already reconciled to God through Christ; or whether Christ has drawn them into his vicarious and saving life of prayer.

Secondly, Christian prayer is a journey and a mission with Jesus Christ in this unbelieving and turbulent world – a journey of prayerful exertions led by his Spirit until his kingdom of righteousness fully arrives.

Thirdly, the experience of Saul of Tarsus on the road to Damascus must serve as both a warning and a great inspiration for those who pray for inclusion. This most famous Pharisee prayed all his life as the law laid down. He claimed he was blameless in his exclusive religious practices before the law! But Saul's prayers only served to reinforce his religious and racial prejudices until, in the heat of his religious hatred, he was driven to exterminate the name of Jesus and his followers, who posed the greatest threat to his religious and racial identity. In fact in all these years Saul never prayed at all until Christ revealed himself to him on his murderous journey to Damascus. What a difference this encounter with Jesus made to Saul – and his praying! For the first time he began to pray (Acts 9:11), for he has been drawn into the company of Jesus 'where all prayer begins and ends'. In this Christ-inspired and informed prayer Saul found himself in a 'new creation' where Jews and Gentiles are reconciled as the children of God; where for the first time Paul understood the meaning of the law, the sinfulness of sin and the redeeming blood of Jesus Christ. The previously unbridgeable gulf between Jews and Gentiles had collapsed.

May God bless this prayer book and the lives of those who use it to the glory of his blessed name!

Revd Ben Tettey
Mytholmroyd
West Yorkshire

Introduction

Inclusion and Diversity have become central issues for churches and communities, bringing joy to many and angst to some. These prayers seek to reflect the needs and concerns of our own time and culture as we come to terms with these issues and embrace the fresh opportunities they open up to us.

But they also seek to draw on the timelessness of our Lord's teaching. For me, it is both salutary and a revelation that so many of the worries and difficulties facing us today have resonances in the stories of the Bible and in Jesus' challenges to the society of the day.

My hope in writing these prayers is that Christians may be helped to express sometimes difficult and troubling concerns in language which is accessible but still prayerful. They are designed principally for use in church and in groups, but may well find a place in the personal prayers of those for whom these issues are all too real.

Readers may also find that the subjects covered here complement other publications, such as *Sermons on Difficult Subjects* (2011), also published by Kevin Mayhew.

Inclusion

Giving and receiving

Generous God,
we love to receive.
Help us to love to give too.
May our experience of receiving good things,
the gift of life, the gift of grace, the gift of your creation,
transform our lives.
And may that lead to a desire to give to others around us
the gifts of listening, learning, loving.
Above all, help us to receive and give, in equal measure,
the hope that your Son showed us.
Amen.

Loving Lord,
you gave us the hope of salvation, the promise of redemption,
the grace of forgiveness.
Let us receive these in gratitude and with thanksgiving.
But strengthen in us the will and the means to help others,
in their spiritual journey, in their physical need,
in their search for truth.
May we love the lost and guide the seeker,
following the way that your Son showed us.
Amen.

God of justice,
help us to use our wealth wisely but extravagantly,
as you showed us with the gifts of your creation.
Let the poor give us the precious capacity to share our good fortune,
model your love and teach us the true route
to a relationship with you,
untouched by status or riches.
Amen.

INCLUSION

Almighty God,
you gave us your Son.
The least we can do is receive him into our hearts.
You gave us your creation.
The least we can do is treat it well.
You gave us hope of eternal life.
The least we can do is believe.
Giving or receiving, may we model your generosity,
show your love.
Amen.

Heavenly Father,
as we thank you for your gifts,
let us love you with our hearts.
As we love you in our hearts,
let us know you in our soul.
Give us strength to so take you into our lives
that we show you in our approach to others.
Give us the desire to so show you in our actions
that we transmit your love and extend your kingdom.
Amen.

Variety in the world

Lord of variety and richness,
bring us to an understanding of difference and diversity,
reflecting your glory, not our prejudice.
Help us to see things through your eyes,
not our short sight.
Create in us the capacity to look for you
in the strange as well as the familiar.
Open our eyes to see, Lord.
Amen.

God of profusion,
you shower us with the fruits of creation
and we often abuse your generosity.
May we always take care
to honour you and respect each other
in our use of all the resources around us.
Help us to pass on your bounty
and safeguard the beauty of the environment
for the benefit of others.
Amen.

Father of all,
let us rejoice in profusion;
let us seek order in confusion.
As societies change, may your presence be plain.
And when communities stagnate,
may your grace create a new way forward,
a fresh start for humankind.
Let grace abound.
Amen.

INCLUSION

Lord of high places,
and God of deep thoughts,
you bring together the physical and the spiritual,
through the incarnation,
in our hearts and minds,
in our going out and our coming in.
Let the sheer range of our experience
be matched by a widening of our understanding
of you and of your kingdom,
in this world and the next.
Amen.

Heavenly Father,
your kingdom is full of variety and abundance.
Help us to recognise its length, depth, height and breadth,
in both this world and the next.
As you entrusted us with your creation,
may we know and believe in the richness of your eternal kingdom,
loving God.
Amen.

Freedom and democracy

Beneficent Lord,
you gave us the freedom to decide and to act,
in accordance with or against your will.
May we have the strength to follow your way,
avoiding temptation to stray
and seeking your forgiveness when we do.
May we so order our affairs
that our freedom can be subject to both your will
and the best rule of law that humankind can devise,
a framework of personal liberty and mutual responsibility.
Amen.

God of grace,
set our hearts and minds at rest,
in the knowledge of your love,
so that in all our doings
we may be fairly treated
and show justice and mercy to others,
as your Son taught us.
May we always know our limitations
as well as seek to explore our ambitions,
provided they are in accordance with your will.
Amen.

God of judgement and justice,
help us to make your kingdom known
through all we do, individually and collectively.
May those in authority and power
seek only to advance the position of the poor and deprived,
serving those least able to help themselves.
Empower and enable the downtrodden
so that they can have the stake in your world
which you promised in your kingdom.
Amen.

INCLUSION

Ever-living Lord,
your freedom gives hope to all;
your love gives peace to all.
May we respond to your grace,
by giving rights and taking responsibility,
by honouring elections and using the vote,
and by respecting the authority of legitimate government,
as your Son did.
Amen.

God of peace,
help us so to manage our affairs
that the rule of law equates to your will for us.
Give to those who govern
the humility to know when their time has come,
to seek re-election
or to step down.
May we learn the lesson of history,
that we get the leaders we deserve,
whereas we can never earn your love,
except by your grace.
Amen.

Faith and faiths

God of all,
let us continue to discern the one true way,
while recognising that others are still on a journey.
May we not presume to map their route to you,
so help us to be sensitive in our mission to them,
not disguising our faith,
but never assuming our superior knowledge.
May all those of faith be guided by you, our beacon,
and through your Son, our compass.
Amen.

Creator God,
bring us gently onto the true path,
through revelation,
through explanation,
through exploration.
But let us honour those on different paths,
praying that we all converge on you.
Let us not be sidetracked by condemning those others,
but help us to model your Son's way,
challenging, asking for and practising
your Son's love for humankind.
Amen.

Lord God,
you uphold the faith that sustains us,
even in the darkest moments.
May others feel that same love,
even if it has been revealed to them in different ways.
Give to all those of faith a special place in your heart,
shown in the compassion of your Son,
as he demonstrated your way.
Amen.

INCLUSION

Father God,
in the midst of joy or sadness,
may we call on the strength of your presence,
to share that happiness or despair.
And may those of different faiths,
and those in search of truth,
see in our response
a glimpse of what can be
and a shared moment of unity,
with us and with you,
universal God.
Amen.

Trusting Lord,
you empower us with the Spirit
to learn your ways and heed your call.
In your Son's mission to humankind
he welcomed Gentiles and Samaritans
to share the feast of your heavenly kingdom.
May we, in our dealings with people of different faiths,
remember the mission of your disciples,
who ensured that the faith survived.
Equip us to express mission today
in fresh ways, in creative ways,
in love.
Amen.

Personal and collective

Lord of one and all,
as individuals we seek your personal love for us;
as community we want your concern for us all.
Keep us safe, personally and collectively,
worshipping you together,
helping our neighbours as ourselves,
and rejoicing in the unity of the Holy Spirit.
Amen.

Father of us all,
look down on your children with grace and forgiveness.
If we stray, bring us home.
If we succeed, let us help the unsuccessful.
If we celebrate, may we share our joy.
Give us the certainty of hope,
not only for ourselves,
but for the community of saints.
Amen.

Heavenly Father, Almighty God,
we praise your generosity in loving us all,
and giving us a second chance through your Son.
May we use the free will you have bestowed on us
to follow his example,
sharing with the poor,
helping the stranger,
welcoming the outcast,
and showing that your love is meant for all,
if we can only accept you into our hearts.
Amen.

INCLUSION

Unifying Lord,
bring together the gifts of individuals
into the collective commonwealth.
May new ideas be shared,
creative strategies combined,
and the will of the whole
be the purpose of the many.
Give us the space to grow
and the desire to join together,
if it be your will.
Amen.

God of grand designs,
show us the way to pool our hope,
so that vision is owned
and purpose shared.
Lift our spirits as you show us the way.
Lighten our burden as you join us on our journey.
Send us out in the knowledge
that we are your disciples.
Amen.

Communicating and obeying

Lord of relationships,
you reached out to us in your Son,
communicating through the incarnation.
May we use the free will you have given us
to respond as well as obey.
May your authority be our reassurance,
your trust our confidence.
Amen.

Almighty God,
may your command be our will,
your need our desire.
In our dealings with others,
let us empower and encourage,
as your Son has equipped us,
to be your willing servants,
to be your true disciples,
to be your loyal advocates,
with the help of the Holy Spirit.
Amen.

Lord of power and might,
help us to obey authority,
even when questioning process.
Help us to command wisely,
even when faced with dissent.
Make us ready to call on others
when we feel unsure.
But give us the confidence
to decide and act,
knowing that you are there
to bind up our wounds
when we fall short.
Amen.

INCLUSION

Almighty God, Heavenly Father,
as you look down on your creation,
give us hope in our world,
as we seek to obey your commandments;
as we take responsibility for managing others;
as we cope with the consequences of our disobedience.
May we never forget
that your Son obeyed your command,
that he suffered for us,
and that by your grace
we have the gift of his teaching
to follow and to guide us.
Amen.

Great Shepherd of the sheep,
may we rejoice in being part of your flock,
heeding your call and following our leaders.
But let us always be mindful
that with obedience comes responsibility,
not only to ourselves,
but to do your will
in enabling others to follow your way,
to bring them to the gatefold,
to rescue the lost
and to care for the lame,
in your name.
Amen.

Roles in family and society

Father of all,
we rejoice in the joys of family.
May we seek always to develop our roles,
as child, parent, carer or relative,
so that we encourage relationship,
model faithfulness,
empower development,
and acknowledge weaknesses.
Give us discernment and humility
as our roles change,
over time and in love.
Amen.

Enabler, Comforter,
give us insight, peace and love,
as we work out our relationships,
with you, with family, with friends.
May we give of ourselves
as we receive from others.
May we share our experience
where relevant and where needed.
May we keep our counsel
when we have nothing to add.
May we play our part,
in community, parish and network,
so that all benefit,
and no one is diminished.
Amen.

INCLUSION

Neighbour, friend, Lord,
may we see you in our street
and not walk by on the other side.
Help us to take responsibility
for our attitude to others.
Give us the skills and the will
to take our roles seriously,
but ourselves lightly,
always seeking to play our part
in reconciling, representing, recognising, rewarding,
so that good is acknowledged
and bad is resisted,
for the benefit of all,
but mostly for your sake.
Amen.

Lord,
give us the confidence to take the reins,
as others fall by the wayside.
May our willingness to share others' burdens
lead to others helping us with ours.
As all things must pass,
so may all things come to fruition,
with all of us playing our part,
at home, at church, in society,
but only with you as our help,
our sole purpose,
and our reason to believe.
Amen.

continued overleaf

God of great things,
help us in the small things,
so that we can grow in hope.
Equip us to lead,
as well as follow.
Inspire us to teach
as well as learn.
May we be good disciples,
fruitful prayers,
loyal friends,
and good Samaritans,
wherever we go,
whoever we are,
in sickness and in health.
Amen.

Competing and collaborating

God of great expectations,
may we always reach for the stars,
even if we end up in the clouds.
May we always seek the best
to disprove that this is the enemy of the good.
May we never give up
if we know that with you everything is possible.
May we never cease to wonder
at the limitlessness of your creation.
Let us work together, Lord,
not try to take you on.
Amen.

Inspiring Lord,
create in us the spark of faith
that can ignite our will.
May that will be harnessed and shared
so that we can achieve together
much more than any individual.
May our competitive instincts
go alongside our collaborative nature,
so that in love and in joy
we can achieve great things for you,
in hope and in charity.
Amen.

Heavenly Father,
lead us into good ways and great ideas
so that we can carry the baton for you,
in sprints as well as in the long haul.
Make us inquisitive and eager
to do your will and make that ours too.

Give us the wisdom to know
when to take the initiative
and when to follow others,
always under you, sovereign Lord.
Amen.

Merciful God,
forgive us when we compete unfairly;
forgive us when we don't compete at all.
Encourage us when we do our very best;
encourage us even when we fail.
Teach us the art of collaboration
through the example of your Son,
who, together with you and the Holy Spirit,
overcame all, even death on the cross,
for our sake.
Amen.

Father of all,
creator of all that is mutually dependent in our universe,
look down on our individual efforts with love.
Give us the will to want to do better
and the skills to put this into practice.
But let us never forget that our strength is yours;
our hope is yours;
we are yours:
in birth, in death,
in mind, body and spirit.
Amen.

Humanity, flora and fauna

Creator God,
you have brought together humankind and nature,
interdependent and vulnerable to each other.
Give to us all, we pray,
a sense of proportion and wonder,
a respect for difference and uniqueness.
Let there be amazement at the power of nature,
as your plan is revealed,
as we see your power,
and as we rediscover our care
for all that is in your world.
Amen.

Lord of all,
help us to love you more,
as we grow in confidence.
Make us more aware of our surroundings,
as we gain knowledge of our place in the world.
Give us space,
but not too much.
Give us resources,
but only what we need.
Give us time,
but only enough to do your will.
Let flora and fauna abound,
so that we can stay around.
Amen.

Heavenly Father,
leave us with grateful hearts
while we enjoy the flora and fauna of your earth,
especially when we find new uses
for scarce resources,

particularly as we create conservation
for endangered species,
always as we take time
to give thanks
for our food and our drink.
Amen.

God of great gifts,
help us to know when to start,
and when to stop,
in our pursuit of knowledge and understanding
of this world in all its variety.
May we see the wisdom of slowing down,
when our eagerness to achieve
overcomes our need to wonder.
And if we ever fail to do this,
stop us in our tracks, Lord.
Let our imprint be small,
leaving yours as large as nature intended.
Amen.

God of north and south – as well as east and west,
safeguard the difference and diversity of the poles,
the wildlife, the habitat,
the sea and the ice.
You have wisely separated penguin from polar bear,
but never let us separate your creatures from their environment.
And may we –
tread softly to protect our dreams;
whisper quietly to honour the silence;
and leave as we found,
gratefully, graciously, gradually.
Amen.

Nature and nurture

Lord of growth and understanding,
teach us to know,
but also to understand.
Help us to learn by doing,
but grow by observing.
Empower us to build on the gifts you have given us,
so that we can grow in our ability
to pass on what we have learnt
and to model what you want us to be,
as your Son did.
Amen.

Creator God,
let us know your ways
by observing your Son.
Let us know what to do
by trusting our priests.
Let us grow in understanding
by learning from our mistakes.
Above all, gracious Lord,
equip us to be,
empower us to do,
and enable us to teach,
whatever you need,
so that, at the last,
our nurture and your nature
have guided our journey
and brought us safely home.
Amen.

Lord of all,
fill us with the knowledge of our nature.
Create in us the capacity for nurture.
Lead us, heavenly Father, lead us,

so that our choices are soundly based,
our decisions forward-focused,
and our guiding light is always your Son,
who restored our nature,
by challenging our nurture,
who welcomed us back
and moved us on,
through your love.
Amen.

Gracious Lord,
give us the humility to learn,
the ability to grasp new knowledge,
and the desire to pass it on.
We know, Lord, that we are all born with great gifts,
but we forget too easily, Lord,
that we need to sharpen and practise our skills
so that all we do
is done in quiet confidence
that your will is done,
that your kingdom will come.
Amen.

Heavenly Father,
look on all we do with favour,
where we honour your gifts
and seek to grow our skills.
Send us the ability to cope,
the confidence to hope,
and the need to grow in you
and you in us.
Amen.

The imprisoned and oppressed

God of freedom,
we pray for those in prison,
the justly imprisoned
as well as those without fault,
the victims of injustice.
For those who have transgressed,
may repentance lead to rehabilitation.
For those wrongly sentenced,
may reconciliation remove bitterness.
And let freedom be the prize
for all who have faith in you.
Amen.

God of justice and mercy,
watch over your servants,
imprisoned by oppression;
caught up in slavery;
trapped in poverty;
kept quiet by censorship;
victimised for their faith;
martyred for their beliefs.
In the restoration of their activities
may their spirits run free,
through the grace of your love,
and the knowledge of your presence.
Amen.

Sovereign Lord,
friend of the oppressed, guardian of the weak,
bring to your people a new beginning,
so that tyrants change their ways,
sinners look for repentance,

INCLUSION

victims forgive,
and your perfect peace is found.
Let there be a new heaven and a new earth,
wherever fear and fighting currently stalk the land.
Amen.

God of grace,
let judgement be in your hands
when we falter and fail
in meeting our responsibilities to you.
And when we let each other down,
through envy, greed and hatred,
may justice be tinged with mercy,
so that wrongdoing is justly punished,
but retribution is left to you,
who knows us better than we know ourselves.
Amen.

Saviour, Lord,
fill us with a sense of justice,
as we seek to follow the rule of law.
But may we follow the example of your Son,
in challenging unfair laws,
in overturning injustice wherever we find it,
in loving the sinner while condemning the sin,
and in never giving up on humanity.
Just as you saw hope in restoring your relationship with us,
may we recognise hope in the future of prisoners,
salvation through the suffering of your Son,
alongside the criminals on the cross.
Amen.

The righteous and the sinner

Father Almighty,
you gave us free will
for us to abuse or use well.
Help us to do right
when we want to do wrong.
Let the righteous flourish
as examples to us all,
as your Son was.
Let the sinners see the errors of their ways:
lead them back to you,
with our help,
under your direction,
in love and hope.
Amen.

God of great expectations,
when we fall short, help us up.
When we don't try, give us 'umph'.
When we overreach ourselves, may we not despair.
Send us out in your name
when we try to take risks for you.
And hold us back from doing harm
when we act selfishly.
Righteous or sinner,
selfless or selfish,
stay with us and keep us on the right path,
loving Lord.
Amen.

INCLUSION

Heavenly Father,
your Son washed away our sins,
but we ask that we remain penitent
for the wrong things we continue to do,
so that we never lose sight of you.
Give us the grace
to understand right from wrong,
but also to love both sinners and righteous,
as your Son showed us on the cross,
as we should do every day,
however hard it is.
Send us out in the power of the Spirit,
to do always what is righteous in your sight.
Amen.

God of might and right,
have mercy on sinners and saints,
because sinners can become saints,
as you have shown us throughout history.
We remember the transgressions
of David, of Solomon, of Saul.
We remember the faint-heartedness of Peter,
of Thomas, of the young lawyer.
We remember the temptations of Jesus by Satan.
May our failings become our strengths,
like Peter, like Paul,
as Jesus has shown us
in bursting the tomb after the trauma of Calvary.
Amen.

continued overleaf

Lord of all hopefulness,
gather us into your calm waters,
especially when the seas have been rough.
Make us aware of your presence,
even when all seems to be lost.
Give us the strength of your Holy Spirit,
in good times and bad,
so that all the righteous
can be encouraged,
and the wicked can be saved:
through your grace,
through the good will of strangers,
and through the continuous prayers
of religious everywhere.
Amen.

The bully and the bullied

Almighty God,
just as you use your power sparingly,
not in anger but justly,
so may we restrain our instinct
to dominate or intimidate.
Give to the bullied resilience,
to the bully restraint,
to the situation peace,
and to the future hope.
Amen.

Lord of all,
bring your healing to the bullied:
may they regain their confidence.
Bring your mercy on the bullies:
may they see the light,
as you show them the way.
May they know the truth,
as you share the life.
At work, at school, at home,
give us the confidence
to take on the bullies
and care for the bullied.
Amen.

God of greatness,
show us how to use our power wisely,
not to intimidate or humiliate.
But let us also strive to find
a way to transform the bullies,
turning Goliaths into Davids,
transforming Sauls into Pauls,
changing Herods into Simeons.

INCLUSION

Everything is possible
to a God who sends his only Son
to be bullied, killed and resurrected.
Amen.

Heavenly Father,
look on our feeble efforts to resist evil
and give us strength.
As your Son took on the forces of sin and death –
and won,
so may we be empowered by your Holy Spirit
to battle against injustice,
oppose oppression,
and seek to establish your kingdom,
here on earth.
Amen.

Essential Lord,
set out for us clear pathways
so that our routes are the right ones.
Help us to recognise blind alleys
and to show the pointlessness of blind rage.
Let our purpose be your purpose
and let us not be deflected
by the desire to dominate others
or to acquiesce in bullying,
whether by individuals or nations.
Let the flame of freedom
be fuelled by your beacon of hope.
Amen.

Atheists and agnostics

God of knowledge and understanding,
you let us all decide
whether to seek you out
and whether to keep on looking
when we search in the wrong places.
May we have the will to continue to explore,
but may we also spare a thought and a prayer
for those who have given up,
for those who never started,
and for those who have rejected you,
even though you have never rejected them.
Amen.

God of hope,
even when the field is apparently lost,
all is not lost;
even when hope is seemingly gone,
faith is waiting to be found.
Bring us hope, Jehovah,
bring us love, Lord God,
and may those who don't believe
never give up the possibility of your presence.
If they think there is probably no God,
it means there possibly is,
and with you all things are possible,
merciful Lord.
Amen.

Lord of love,
may atheists and agnostics have their say,
without attracting our alarm or anger.
But may atheists and agnostics
also acknowledge our right to believe,
whatever our denomination or faith.

INCLUSION

You are far too important
for us to tick off or cross out
as a lifestyle option or an accepted fact.
People have fought and died for you,
so religion deserves challenge
as well as respect,
exploration rather than blind obedience.
Amen.

Lord God,
help us to understand
that knowing you is loving you;
that not knowing you is depriving you of love,
but not stopping your love for us.
Give us time to grow
and time to know.
And may you never give up on us,
as you showed through your Son,
our Saviour, Jesus Christ.
Amen.

God of grandeur,
it sometimes seems that you are too great to ignore,
yet still people do – and we occasionally do too.
Give courage to those with belief
to admit to moments of doubt.
But let atheists see that they can doubt too,
and may agnostics recognise the creativity of doubt,
so that sparks of belief can ignite the embers of faith,
to your glory – and theirs too.
Amen.

Leadership and discipleship

Lord of leadership,
encourage all who try to be your disciples.
May we learn your ways by listening to your Son.
And may we see how his disciples were challenged,
but also were led by example,
and then passed on your word
through their pastoral ministry,
as well as their preaching and teaching.
Give us the right leaders,
so that we can be good disciples.
Amen.

Heavenly Father,
be a beacon of hope
and a shining star;
a plumb-line
and a leading light.
From the day of your Son's birth
to his lonely agony on the cross,
to the resurrection and ascension,
we were never let down,
unlike you,
never abandoned,
unlike him.
Lead us, Heavenly Father,
to the ends of the earth – and beyond.
Amen.

Amazing Lord,
God of justice and power,
let your will prevail
through love and relationship.
Let your love bring us through
and your Holy Spirit guide us on our way.
May we never let a stone stay unturned
in our efforts to share your love with others,
before you welcome us home.
Amen.

God of mission,
send us out in your name:
to be good disciples;
to show true leadership;
to be good learners as well as teachers;
to wrestle with you,
and with each other,
if it brings us to see the truth,
the way and the life
that your Son gave us.
Amen.

Lord of all,
make us and break us,
take us and remake us,
in your image,
in our imagination,
in our action,
and in our person.
Let your Holy Spirit work on us,
let your Son shape us,
and may you judge us.
Amen.

Growing old

Lord of light and might,
be with us through the years;
be with us through the tears.
May joy be long-lasting
and memories be fond;
and let those who come after
know those who went before.
Bring comfort in old age
and hope for years to come.
Amen.

God of heaven and earth,
we give thanks for experience,
for the gift of achievement
as well as the sorrow of loss.
May we always learn from failure,
as much as we delight in success.
Bring wisdom with age
and a love for the future
greater than longing for the past.
Be with us through the years, we pray.
Amen.

Lord of grace and mercy,
may we grow old with dignity
and let go with equanimity.
Help us to pass on rather than hang on,
whatever our particular strengths.
May we value our relationships
with friends, family and acquaintances,
being good neighbours and loyal partners,
in business, church, community and street,
always ready to be true to ourselves,
but also to you, eternal Father.
Amen.

INCLUSION

God of hope,
may we view each day as a gift,
each hour a jewel,
each moment an opportunity.
Help us to value time as a friend,
not an enemy to be chased.
As we grow in our love for you,
let us seek to make a difference to this world,
even as we set our eyes on the next.
Amen.

God of all ages,
let us embrace the process
of growing older and wiser.
Give us humility and charity
alongside our desire for security.
Cast out fear for the future
in giving us a sense of the past.
Let peace reign and hope take hold,
from this day forward.
Amen.

Mental health

Compassionate Lord,
bring us an understanding of your mind,
a glimpse of your truth,
which will help us to know
the extent of your love.
Embrace, we pray, the needs of those
who do not see clearly,
who find it difficult to relate to others,
and who go through phases of illness
in mind, in spirit, in relationship.
Bring calm and healing to troubled minds.
Amen.

Suffering servant,
make all things new for us,
and especially for those with mental illness.
Make us compassionate through our engagement
and sensitive to the vulnerabilities
of those who are sick.
May we always see the person
behind the behaviour,
just as we see you
behind your creation,
knowing what is of you
and what is our contribution,
our value added or taken away.
Amen.

Lord of health and wholeness,
look down, we pray,
on those who struggle with life.
Set them free from despair
through the glimpse of the hope you bring.

INCLUSION

However it seems through the mist of hurt,
let your love dispel the cloud of unknowing
and restore a right relationship
with self, with you, with all around.
Amen.

God of great expectations,
lift the spirits of all who suffer
from mental strife,
from guilt and pain,
from hate and insecurity.
Open the curtains to our soul
and let the light shine in.
Dispel doubt and fear
from the hearts of those who find it difficult
to face the next day
with the confidence you can inspire.
Amen.

All-embracing God,
you understand the turmoil of those
whose mental state is a worry to others.
Release the energy of hope
in those who see only danger.
Bring self-knowledge and sensitive care
to the fragile and vulnerable in mind and spirit.
Above all, Lord, create in all of us, we pray,
the capacity to care, the patience to persevere,
as your Son did – and still does.
Amen.

Racism

God of diversity and difference,
draw out from those with evil intent
any traces of racism.
Replace hatred of other colours and cultures
with understanding, respect, knowledge,
so that through love shown to them
they may model a new way,
a new dawn, a fresh start,
as the Good Samaritan showed us
and your Son told us.
Amen.

Lord of all,
you have given us variety and choice,
so that through your own free will
we can acknowledge or deny you.
If, by your grace, we come to know you,
let all racist thought be swept away,
through the all embracing love
which you have shared with us
and shared with all.
Amen.

King of kings and Lord of lords,
you have come down to be with us
in your Son, who shared our humanity
alongside his divinity.
Let us model ourselves on his acceptance
of Jew and Gentile, man and woman,
master and servant, slave and free.
May that spirit of being one in Christ
be made obvious in all we do and say;
and may we confront racism where we find it,
as your Son did.
Amen.

INCLUSION

Shepherd and servant,
we ask your forgiveness
where we say or suggest
anything that others find offensive or insensitive,
especially where racism is lurking,
and where thoughtlessness can be interpreted as prejudice.
You have made us creatures of our upbringing,
but your Son taught us to break free
from wrong thoughts and sinful outcomes.
Give us strength to resist evil and do good,
by loving you and loving our neighbour too.
Amen.

Lord of love,
make us all less fearful of the different,
more accepting of the stranger,
and intolerant of all that gives room for racism to flourish.
Send us out to spread the word
of your universal love,
without condition, without barrier,
without fear of appearance
or taint of discrimination.
May we be all for one,
our Saviour, Jesus Christ.
Amen.

Redundancy and unemployment

God of labour and rest,
you showed us that we are entitled to rest,
as you were on the seventh day.
But help us to come to terms with enforced rest,
with losing our employment.
Give us the hope to find a new job,
but also new ways to use our time wisely
and, more than anything,
to know you better.
Amen.

Merciful Father,
who loves the labourer worthy of his hire,
look with favour on those who lose their jobs,
yet who have so much to offer.
Give them the skill and the determination
to demonstrate their worth,
whether at home or in the community,
whether seeking new employment
or working for your kingdom.
May we never feel redundant
from our work for you
and renew our trust in your goodness.
Amen.

Saving Lord,
your redeeming love has brought us new life.
Whether working or seeking work,
whether training or retired,
may we never let up in our work for you,
and may we never make your name redundant
in our lives.
Amen.

Lord God,
bring to those who seek your name
the same endeavour as if it was their job.
May we never seek to deny you
by withdrawing our prayers and praise.
And may you always support our efforts
to find new employment
if redundancy is forced upon us.
May an economic recession
be an opportunity to rekindle the fire of our faith.
Amen.

Almighty God,
may we never lose heart,
even if we lose our livelihood.
Bring us ingenuity and hope
to find a new way forward,
as your Son taught us to do
in restoring our relationship with you.
Bring to the unemployed
a true appreciation of a life well lived,
through prayer and service,
even when jobs are scarce
and resources are low.
Amen.

Youth culture

Heavenly Father,
in bringing us life, you give us youth.
Pour your blessings on the next generation,
as they find their way in your world.
Let them make mistakes
but protect them from harm.
Let them challenge our assumptions
but learn from the past.
Let them use the public space
but not intimidate others.
We ask this through the one who is forever young,
Jesus Christ.
Amen.

God who makes all things new,
may we be tolerant
of things we don't like in the young.
Help us to think of our youth,
when we were making our way in an adult world.
Help us to give encouragement
rather than find reasons to blame.
And where the music causes pain,
or behaviour falls short,
let us remember how the prodigal son
was welcomed home,
forgiving Father.
Amen.

Exuberant, extravagant God,
bring creativity and a sense of wonder
to our young people,
in their lives and in their hearts.
May we all listen to the voice of youth,
uncut, unvarnished, as it is.

INCLUSION

May the power of listening
model the power of talking,
so that we may all grow
in love, in truth, in relationship
with each other and, above all, with you, Lord.
Amen.

God of truth and honesty,
may the insights of youth
be shared in our churches.
Let the love of learning
be matched by inspirational teaching,
at home, at school, and in church.
Let youth ride out
and wisdom march on
where you are in the lead.
Amen.

Sensational Lord,
surround the youth of today
with the cloak of your love,
so that no matter if they stumble,
no matter if they offend,
they are being true to themselves,
true to each other,
and true to you.
May they strive for peace,
even if their efforts are noisy.
Help us not to ape their ways or interests
but be ready to learn from their insights.
Amen.

Worry

God of peace and calm,
watch over us in times of struggle,
when everything seems against us,
when we feel we are letting ourselves down
and not doing justice to you.
Take our cares on your broad shoulders
and bring us the focus
to do your will
and cast our worries aside.
Thank you, Lord.
Amen.

O God who cares,
take our worries and shake them,
so that we see ourselves as we really are.
Take our lives and shake them,
so that we see who you truly are.
May we remain on the one true path
and not be distracted by worries or temptations,
or by the fear of doing wrong,
when we are seeking to do the right thing.
May our risks be your risks, Lord,
so that together we can get things right.
Amen.

INCLUSION

Teaching Lord,
enable us to pray without guilt;
teach us to share without resentment.
Enable us to challenge without fear;
teach us to love without lusting.
Enable us to give without receiving;
teach us to live without worrying.
Enable us to thank without condition;
teach us to follow you without questioning,
enabling Lord.
Amen.

Heavenly Father,
we pray for the grace you have freely shown
to remove our fears and worries
about the things we cannot change,
about the concerns which you have lifted from us,
about the issues which do not really matter.
But where we face real difficulty,
big decisions and tough times,
help us to discern the right path,
knowing you are with us all the way.
Amen.

Gracious Lord,
create in us, we pray,
a way to deal with worry
which helps us to face the big issues
without being dragged down by selfish concerns.
Give us the faith in hope to see us through
and the hope of faith to bring us home.
Amen.

Innovators/completer finishers

Creator God,
you are the Alpha and the Omega,
the beginning and the end.
We thank you for all the innovators
who have been inspired, by your creative spirit,
to extend, adapt and interpret your creation.
May that spark bring new developments
which are true to your founding heart,
new ways that honour you.
Amen.

God of great events,
we thank you for those who generate ideas
and those who follow them through.
May we have the humility to know
that most of us cannot do both.
May we be content that different gifts
brought together by your grace
may flourish in teams of people
who share the same vision.
May your Son's disciples
be our warning and our guide.
Amen.

Lord of lords, King of kings,
let dreamers dream and imaginations soar,
as the sheer dazzling potential of your creation
inspires many to invent and innovate.
May those with project management skills
complete and finish the big ideas,
but may we all do so,
knowing that our co-operation

INCLUSION

will only work by the grace
of the one who created all things,
through Jesus Christ, our Lord.
Amen.

God of small things,
help us to understand the power of the mustard seed
to grow and flourish as a large bush despite its small beginnings.
May we look for ways of nurturing the seeds of hope
amidst the seeds of destruction,
so that the good earth you have provided
may last and flourish
and we play our part
as good stewards and gentle encouragers
of new growth and fresh fruits.
Amen.

Lord of all hopefulness,
give us the will and the means
to use the mind you have given us
to generate new insights, new ideas.
May we also have the ingenuity
to see these ideas through to fruition,
just as you restored your relationship with humankind
through the greatest project ever,
your Son becoming human,
living among us, bringing the good news
of our salvation through his sacrifice and your grace,
a mission begun, continued and ended in you.
Amen.

Hot and cold

God of heat and light,
give us an appreciation
of the warmth of a fire in winter
and the cool of shade in summer.
May those who live in hot climates
be blessed with sufficient rain;
and those who live in temperate areas
feel the sun on their face in between the cloud.
Thank you for all the benefits of heat and cold.
Amen.

God of balance and exchange,
let us give thanks for contrasts:
for the blessings of warmth
and the refreshment of cold.
But let us be mindful of extremes,
which explorers have experienced
during centuries of pushing back the frontiers
of height and depth, of danger and difficulty.
May we always appreciate the efforts of others
who test boundaries for our comfort and safety.
Amen.

Heavenly Father,
you brought us sunshine and rainfall,
but also the challenge of drought and flood.
You gave us snows and rivers,
but also the challenge of ice and avalanche.
You created desert and ice cap,
but also the challenge of thirst and frostbite.
Challenge us, change us, but keep us safe.
Amen.

God our refuge,
stretch our comprehension of extremes,
so that we can truly appreciate
the gift of warmth, not the distress of burning,
the refreshment of cooling, not the danger of freezing.
Let us respond and be glad
in the balm and variety
of the temperatures you give us.
Amen.

Maker of heaven and earth,
bringer of heat and cold,
we thank you for the preservation of life,
through the blend of heat and light,
of water and wind.
In all the changes and chances of life,
let us celebrate the sheer variety of your creation,
the great blessing that this world provides,
the essential goodness of your love.
Amen.

Solitude and gregariousness

Father, Son and Holy Spirit,
you are indivisible yet stand alone.
Make us appreciate the importance
of solitude and community
in our lives and in our hearts.
We ask this through the love of the one who sets us free
yet brings us home,
your Son, our Saviour,
Jesus Christ.
Amen.

Father of all,
we owe you everything in life,
our hopes, our dreams, our loves.
May we always respect those who choose solitude,
as the desert fathers did and as hermits still do.
But may we be tolerant of those who need others,
to talk to, to complain to, to listen to, to command or obey.
May we have the right balance in our lives,
in families as well as friendships.
Amen.

Lord God,
when I am alone I still need you.
When I am in company let me not forget you.
Help us to be sensitive
to the lonely who always feel alone
and to those who desperately want their space,
but are never free from the demands of others,
as you must feel sometimes,
gracious Lord.
Amen.

INCLUSION

Saving God,
when we are all alone
bring us out of the depths of despair
by showing us how to hope.
Let the gifts of the gregarious
be showered on the lonely.
We are a community in communion
when we worship you
and share the Eucharist,
in thanks and praise.
Alone, together,
in peace, in partnership,
we are yours, Lord.
Amen.

God of mercy,
we thank you for the unifying force of prayer,
across borders, across generations.
Make prayer our delight and our guide,
when together, when apart,
in good times and bad.
May the light of the world
be a beacon for creative solitude
as well as community cohesion,
throughout our lives.
Amen.

Music and musicians

God of soul and spirit,
lift our hearts through music and song
and bring me to tears
in joy as well as sadness.
We ask for your blessings on music and musicians,
on all who feed our soul
and touch our spirit
with sacred music,
the beat of angels' wings,
and the sound of the spheres.
Amen.

Lord of life and rhythm,
stretch our senses through music and movement,
in the way we respond to music
and through the gifts of your great goodness.
May our spirits soar
as the notes of music and musicians,
sacred and secular,
set our minds free
and our imaginations running.
Amen.

God of peace and perfection,
may the melody and harmony of music
connect with the pull of our heartstrings
and the fondness of memories,
from 'madeleine moments'
to loves lost and won.
Set us searching for these
through chords and choruses,
through instruments and voices,
always remembering the origins
of their creative spark.
Amen.

INCLUSION

God of glory,
may we appreciate the silence between notes,
the calm between the storms,
and the light in the midst of darkness.
Let music refine our sense of you,
as it defines our understanding of ourselves.
We thank you for the inspiration
of composition
and the mastery of musicians in their craft.
Amen.

Searching Lord,
may we respond to your open arms
through the spirit of music
as well as the power of the word.
In worship and praise
let us sing out our love for you.
And in the gifts you have bestowed on musicians
may we see your love at work,
in note and form,
in tempo and timing.
Amen.

Animals and pets

Loving Lord,
we thank you for the creatures of your world,
domesticated or wild, large and small.
Help us to treat them well,
as they are our neighbours too,
reminding us of the cycle of life
and the consequences of mortality.
Bring out the best in us
as we care for our animals and pets,
we pray.
Amen.

God of companionship,
what a friend we have in Jesus,
born in a stable shared with animals,
showing care and concern for them
in life and in death.
Help us to model good practice
in animal husbandry,
so that we can look your Son in the face
in giving an account of ourselves.
Amen.

Lord of land and sea,
may the creatures of your world
live in harmony with humankind,
bringing out the best in us
and nurturing the animal kingdom.
Set our standards high
so that we may give a good example
to our families, to our fellow humans,
and to future generations.
Amen.

Lord of love,
may we show in our love of pets
a special bond between us and the rest of your creation,
in the knowledge that we are all one
in sharing the benefits of life,
the environment and your world.
We thank you for the special place of pets
in our lives and in our hearts.
Amen.

God of creation,
we ask for your blessings on the animal kingdom,
for the joy that animals give us,
for the food that they provide,
for the milk and wool they offer us.
And when we plan our way of life
or changes in our environment,
help us to think carefully about
the impact of our actions
on the fauna and flora around us,
and pause (for prayer and thought) . . .
Amen.

Rural and urban

God of life,
bless our human habitations,
in city and country, town or village.
Look down with favour on our land
and the places where all your people live.
We thank you for the sheer variety
in our landscape, in our city streets,
in the cultures and languages across the world.
Amen.

Lord of land and sea,
let our hearts leap and our spirits soar
as we behold a rainbow in the sky.
And may the beauty of sunset
be as glorious over our seas and hills,
as over our cityscapes and beautiful bridges.
May our built environment echo the natural world,
so that we can be proud of both.
And wherever we live,
may we appreciate and protect our environment.
Amen.

Heavenly Father,
thank you for the countryside,
for the flowers, trees and crops
as well as the rolling hills and winding streams.
Whether we live in town or country,
help us to appreciate the variety of our world.
Bring us a glimpse of heaven
in hedgerow and copse,
a scent of eternity
in honeysuckle and lavender.
Amen.

INCLUSION

Generous God,
you gave us resources to build with
and the skills to design and construct.
Bring imagination, flair and inspiration
to the processes of designing and building.
Give us the good sense
to complement building and landscape,
to construct with community and neighbour in mind.
And let us live in harmony with both.
Amen.

Enduring Father of all,
send us out in this world
conscious of our responsibilities to each other and your world.
Bring us home having done our best
to blend old and new, tradition and innovation.
In our daily round, our common task,
may we always recognise the impact, for good or ill,
on the environment we pass through,
as well as the environment in which we live.
Amen.

Sport and leisure

Almighty God,
you taught us to work hard and then rest.
Help us to work with good humour
and to take our fun seriously.
May we rejoice in active relaxation,
stretching the mind, body and spirit
which you have given to us.
May we exercise well and often
as we also pray,
through your Son, Jesus Christ.
Amen.

God of amazing grace,
help us to treat our body as our spirit,
exercising both regularly and routinely,
enjoying each and celebrating both.
We ask for your blessings on all sport and recreation,
at Olympic level and in schools,
on village greens and in backyards,
in great stadia and on local recreation grounds.
May we support teams and admire excellence.
Amen.

All-knowing God,
you know the laws of Scrabble
and the rules of cricket.
You have seen many interpretations of the off-side rule
and the murky etiquette of the scrum.
May the principle of fair play in games and sport
loom large in daily living,
so that we can live in harmony,
even when we work in competition.
Amen.

God of fulfilment,
may we fill our leisure time
with proper rest and energetic enjoyment.
Give us purpose in our relaxation
to balance intensity in our work.
Your Son taught us the importance of calm and stillness,
even in the face of challenge and danger.
May we seek to emulate him
who walks and exercises by our side,
sometimes carrying us, always listening to us,
your Son, our Saviour,
Jesus Christ.
Amen.

Lord of purpose and growth,
in all our endeavours give us trust:
trust in our ability to persevere;
trust in our judgement and timing;
trust in our preparation and planning;
and above all, trust in your guiding light,
in this world and the next,
to inspire and encourage us,
to spur us on and hold us back,
to bring us safely home,
in this world and the next.
Amen.

Reading and writing

God of scripture,
give your creative spirit to all who write;
may they capture the truth they seek to explain.
Illuminate their thoughts with the light of love,
and provide them with the right words
to express their thoughts and feelings.
Amen.

Creator God,
help us to read into the minds of those who write.
May we glimpse their insights
as we rejoice in their words.
Let the things we read and learn
inform our thinking
and lead us to balanced views
and deeper thoughts,
as well as enjoyable moments.
Let your love shine
through the prism of the printed page
and the magic of the screen.
Amen.

Liberating Lord,
set our minds free from routine thoughts
as we enter the world of imagination,
either our own as we seek the creative spark,
or through the minds of others,
as we read their work or see their vision.
Save us from going through the motions,
as we engage our inmost yearnings.
Amen.

INCLUSION

Lord of spirit and truth,
surround our thoughts and hopes
with meditation and contemplation.
As we seek to make sense of the world,
through poetry and prayer,
through word and deed,
through music and song,
may your spirit spark
exploration of the gift of imagination,
in writer, reader and viewer alike.
What a wonderful world!
Amen.

Heavenly Father,
may we write on a wing and a prayer,
as we explore your world
through the imagination of our hearts and minds.
Bring us the ability to interpret and test,
through our reading and writing.
May your Holy Bible be the fount of wisdom
and the backdrop to all our musing.
And may the writers of today
acknowledge their debt – and ours – to your Word.
Amen.

Communities and networks

God of communion,
may we see you in others
so that we may love our neighbour.
May we believe you in others
so that we can learn your wisdom.
May we love you in others
so that we may learn your grace.
Amen.

Loving and nurturing Lord,
set our sights high and our walls low
as we reach out to you through others.
May our network be your community too.
Let relationships thrive as we share our interests.
Let understanding grow
as different minds address an issue.
Give us the desire to work together
in a demanding common task.
Amen.

God of connections,
may the power of human instincts
always be more powerful than the technology that serves us.
Bring us to a proper realisation
of the potential and the limitations
of a community of souls,
dedicated to each other, and to you.
May peace reign and love rule.
Amen.

INCLUSION

Lord of life,
bring us a true sign of your presence
through community and communion.
May we learn by reaching out,
build relationships with others through knowing you,
and create a better place
by the interchange of thought
and the benefit of debate.
May we truly worship
when we gather together,
in prayer and praise,
to hear your word and give thanks.
Amen.

Father of all,
gather us together for mutual support,
but also for challenge and change.
May we be better prepared,
in this world and the next,
when we meet and greet,
share and care,
value our difference and diversity.
Never let the potential of technology
deprive us of human interaction,
the glue of community
and the basis of humanity
in the world you have created,
saved by your Son,
Jesus Christ.
Amen.

Diversity

Ethnicity

God of great diversity,
let us rejoice in the differences in your world,
symbolised in cultures and races.
May we all have pride in our own ethnicity,
while respecting that of others,
in our country and abroad,
in our places of worship
and in our communities.
Amen.

Lord of Jew and Gentile,
your Son taught us how to expect the best of others,
irrespective of race, class or gender.
We remember how he was rejected as the Messiah of the Jews,
yet brought salvation to us all.
Samaritans, tax collectors, Canaanite women:
all were brought to him by faith,
and he reciprocated by welcoming them
into his kingdom, your kingdom, our kingdom.
Amen.

Serene and sensitive Lord,
you send us out in your name,
to explore your will in all its diversity.
Open our eyes to the delights of difference,
showing us how ethnicities can unite
as well as divide our world.
May Christ our cornerstone
be the uniting factor
in supporting the span of humankind
in your world, our home.
Amen.

DIVERSITY

Great and glorious King of kings,
your empire embraces all creeds, colours and cultures.
May we see the best in each other
under your rule.
May we show the best of ourselves
in honouring the difference.
May we share the best of your love
in our dealings with others.
Let us not cry for our beloved country,
but laugh with joy at its richness.
Amen.

Sovereign Lord,
let us search out our feelings
about other ethnicities.
Let us reflect on how those feelings
have changed;
need to change;
are affected by our faith.
Help us to be honest, open, and true,
to ourselves, to others, and, above all,
to the one who has taught us
how to love our neighbour as ourselves,
Jesus Christ.
Amen.

Religion

Gracious God,
you taught us how to love you
by sending your Son to be alongside us.
In all the mystery and majesty of your word,
may we never forget
the origins of that creation
begun, continued and extended in you.
Your Son has brought us close,
but let us bridge that short gap
between us and eternity,
by turning to the one who brings us
the peace of God which passes all understanding,
your Son, our Saviour,
Jesus Christ.
Amen.

Lord,
it sometimes seems that there is too much religion in the world
and not enough faith.
Yet in religion you have given us the capacity
to worship you reverently and joyfully,
knowing that you hear our prayer
and receive our praise.
Help us to be
a bit more faithful in our religion,
a bit less religious in our faith.
Amen.

DIVERSITY

Almighty God,
you give us the opportunity and the desire to worship you.
Let us not only feel the need to do so,
but the desire to show our love and praise.
In choosing to follow your Son,
we do so with joy in our heart.
In trusting you, let us respect
the hope that others have also,
even though they may express that faith in different ways.
Amen.

God of power and might,
we acknowledge you to be our king.
Bring us greater knowledge and understanding of your kingdom
and also of the rival claims to that kingdom.
Through our faith, let us open doors rather than close them;
through your promises, let us be tested and not found wanting.
Strengthen us in our faith
and stretch us to express that faith in fresh ways.
Amen.

Lord of all,
build in us the blessings of baptism;
create in us the confidence of confirmation;
equip us to engage in evangelism;
and never let us stray
from being partners in your mission,
to humankind, neighbour and friend,
stranger and outcast, young and old.
Amen.

Gender

God of love,
you have given us male and female
to bring us companionship,
to bring us children,
to bring happiness and joy.
But we ask for your healing hand
upon clashes and difficulties between men and women,
upon misunderstandings which get out of hand,
and upon the bereaved in their loss of a loved one.
Be our companion and guide,
in good times and bad.
Amen.

Creator God,
may gender be a reason to rejoice,
not a reason to judge.
We ask for your blessings
on all who are unsure of their gender,
that there may be understanding and respect
for differences and confusion.
And may the battle of the sexes
be reserved for the theatre and film,
rather than the home and the hearth.
Amen.

Gracious God,
'vive la différence' we say,
and for which we give you thanks.
In all our lives
we are blessed, challenged and affected
by relationships across genders and
from birth to death;
from love to hate;
from hurt to health.

May we experience the richness of those relationships
and learn from mistakes made.
Amen.

Inclusive God,
may those who relate more to their own gender
be able to share and show their love
without judgement or accusation.
Let loyalty and fidelity be the true mark of love,
and the real test, in life as in our faith,
as you showed in remaining loyal to us,
even when we turned our back on you,
forgiving Lord.
Amen.

Lord of life,
set our sights high in seeking and showing love.
Let us learn from your Son the need
to listen
to enquire
to teach
to challenge
to forgive.
But not
to judge
to ignore
to dismiss
to fight back
to betray.
Be a kind teacher for a hard task.
Amen.

Sexuality

God of the senses,
we thank you for the delights of making love,
for the feelings you have given us,
as well as the means to express them.
We have been given these gifts
to use wisely and well,
though sometimes with abandon.
Let us rejoice and be glad.
Amen.

Heavenly Father,
look down with favour on those you have created,
the diversity and difference,
as well as the common bonds of humanity.
May the joys of sexual attraction
be directed aright,
not just according to human rules,
but by your divine guidance,
so that we can honour
the fruits of your creation,
even when the norms of humankind are broken.
Amen.

Great God of hope,
may our sexual encounters
be full of your grace.
May our lives fulfil expectations
and confound experience.
May we learn from loss
and value faithfulness.
Let our relationships reflect our faith,
in our desire to be worthy of you
in our honouring of partners.
Amen.

Lord God,
we rejoice in our sexuality,
whatever our preferences.
Help us to be true to ourselves,
but remain true to you.
In our community, at work and at home,
let us choose our lifestyle carefully,
and honour our partners faithfully.
Bring good out of our relationships
and help us not to hurt or be hurt.
Amen.

Lord of lords,
we are your unworthy servants,
but make us worthy of your love,
not only in our prayers and praise,
but in our lives,
the way we love,
the way we trust,
the way we work,
the way we are,
the way we thank you,
through Jesus Christ, our Lord.
Amen.

Disability

God of strength and weakness,
you showed your vulnerability
through your Son's mission to earth,
his acceptance of suffering,
his openness to the needs of others.
May his example to the rich and able,
and his reaching out to the meek and the lame,
give heart to all,
challenging the strong and uplifting the weak.
Amen.

God of triumph and tragedy,
may we all see a glass half full,
in counting our blessings
and knowing our gifts.
May we seek to make the most of those gifts
and take our social needs in our stride.
May our impairments make us stronger
and our disabilities spur us to overcome them,
by perseverance, by determination,
and by your grace.
Amen.

Enabling Lord,
send us out in the power of your Spirit
to live, to work, to play and to love
without self-consciousness or fear.
Let our frailties draw on your strength
and our strength inspire others.
Let us be a community of enablers,
gracious Lord.
Amen.

DIVERSITY

God of hope,
bring to us all your Son's inclusive words,
in inviting all to join him
in a kingdom free of prejudice.
Bring to us his inclusive heart,
in bringing your word to Jew and Gentile,
rich and poor, able-bodied and disabled.
May we all learn from those in need
and give in return our time as much as our resources.
Amen.

Lord of all time,
lift up hearts and spirits
when misfortune strikes.
Bring wholeness in place of emptiness
when despair takes over.
Bring healing to ailments
when faith is evident.
May disabilities be transformed
into strength of spirit
which overcomes all and inspires many.
Amen.

Height and weight

Almighty God,
your Son experienced the highs and lows of mortal life;
let our lives be richer for his sacrifice
high on the cross, borne down by his own weight,
but redeeming us all by his precious blood.
Let us be sensitive to the significance
of height and weight,
in our lives,
in giving you thanks.
Amen.

Heavenly Father,
you have made us all shapes and sizes,
part of life's rich pattern and diversity.
But never let us think
that by being tall or short,
fat or slim, heavy or lightweight,
we are somehow better or inferior.
Judge us, Lord, by our spirit,
our faith and our works,
as we seek to be part of your kingdom.
Amen.

Lord of gifts and gaps,
may we be long on patience;
let us be short with pomposity.
May we be great on prayer;
let us be miserly on anger.
May we be weighed down with generosity;
let us be light on seriousness.
Give us the mystery of a miracle
and the depth of a parable.
Amen.

DIVERSITY

God of greatness,
may we strive to know the extent of your greatness,
without ever really knowing.
May we seek the depth of your wisdom,
without fully comprehending.
Give us a glimpse of eternity
without revealing all,
until we meet in your kingdom,
face to face.
Amen.

Lord of great weight,
we know that we can never see infinity,
just as we can never understand eternity.
But in our appreciation of height and weight,
never let us lose sight of the essence
of mind and matter,
of personality and character,
rather than seeking to measure or weigh them.
Amen.

Age

Lord of all the years,
let time be our friend, not our enemy.
Help us to grow up safely,
grow old gracefully,
and always grow in faith and understanding of you.
You gave us Old Testament and New,
so that we might fully appreciate
the lengths to which you have gone
to save us from ourselves and for you,
through your Son, Jesus Christ.
Amen.

Ageless God,
who has been since before time,
who created where there was nothing,
and who will be forever,
look down on our world
and reclaim it as yours,
through the actions and teaching
of your Son's disciples through the ages,
stemming from your intervention in the world,
through your Son, our Saviour,
Jesus Christ.
Amen.

God of grand designs,
when you gave us the world,
you did not leave it ticking by itself,
unchecking clock-like laws.
We give thanks for your constant watch
over the varied futures of your people,
our waywardness and faithfulness,
our disobedience and discipleship.
We thank you that you did not give up on us.
Amen.

Sovereign Lord,
give us hope down all our years,
so that we can make sense of what has gone
and prepare for what will be.
May the vulnerability of childhood
become the energy of youth,
and the responsibility of parenthood
become the wisdom of age.
May the generations not always see eye to eye,
but may they always learn from one another.
Amen.

God of memory and moment,
help us to have fond memories
of people and places we have known,
of our successes and failures,
of our lives and losses.
May age bring out the best of those memories,
and push to one side
the negativity and resentment,
forgiving but not forgetting
any hurt we may have suffered from others.
We ask this in the name
of the one who forgave and forgives,
Jesus Christ.
Amen.

Wealth and poverty

Lord of creation,
you have given us infinite riches
in the cosmos and in our world.
Help us to appreciate that your resources
are for everyone, not just for a few.
Where we find unfairness,
may we seek to change it;
where we see hunger,
may we respond to need.
Let us be your agents
in sharing what we have
with those without their fair share
of what is yours.
Amen.

God of the poor,
may we learn from the spirit of those with less
and not aspire to become those with more, at their expense.
Let us reach out,
not only with practical help,
but with joyful hearts.
Let us become partners in your enterprise
in linking humanity to each other and to you,
with the help of your Son,
Jesus Christ.
Amen.

Lord of free will,
make us more aware of what we should do
to honour you with our heart and with our possessions.
Do we have to give away one to gain the other?
Or can we commit to you
as well as making our possessions work for you?
As we follow on from the young lawyer who asks your Son,
may we reflect and make the right choices in your sight.
Amen.

DIVERSITY

Saving Lord,
let us know how best we can respond
to your generosity in creating our world and seeking your Son.
How can we ever repay you?
We pray for guidance
as we meet poverty;
as we see great wealth;
as we become aware of inequality;
as we experience overwhelming hospitality,
often from those with least.
Turn us upside down
in our expectations and in our responses.
Amen.

Sovereign God,
when you bring us the days of wine and roses,
may we rejoice but also reflect,
so that we do not lose sight
of the needs of the world.
May the wealth that we have
be directed at the poverty that is always with us,
not because of guilt and shame,
but because you have shown us the way
to share, to sacrifice,
to include rather than exclude.
Amen.

Beauty and utility

Lord of truth and beauty,
we know that you have created all things,
seen and unseen, known and unknown.
We give thanks for all that is beautiful,
but also everything that is useful.
Where both go hand in hand, thank you.
Where we find the one or the other,
we nevertheless praise your handiwork, Lord.
Amen.

All-knowing, all-seeing God,
help us to see the value of form and purpose.
We see the glories of beauty,
in people, in places,
in nature, in the universe,
as we give thanks.
In all that works and serves its purpose,
let us always look for beauty in utility,
the divine purpose in your world.
Amen.

Glorious God, Lord of time and space,
let us see your purpose in all your works,
in our hearts as well as in our bodies,
in nature as well as in man-made creations.
Let us not dismiss a person or an artefact
because of their appearance,
and let us not be blinkered by looks,
if the heart is evil,
or the purpose wrong.
Bring us judgement in our eyes
as well as in our mind.
Amen.

DIVERSITY

Severe and sensitive Lord,
open our eyes to truth and meaning
as well as beauty and form.
We cannot assume that all is well
if things look good or someone smiles.
Give us the gift of gentle enquiry
and the meaning of small,
unremembered acts of kindness and love.
Amen.

God of great gifts,
let us rejoice in the great purpose you have for us,
and also the means you have given us
to carry out your mission.
Let us always be aware of the greatest story ever told,
in how we lead our lives.
The beauty of Bethlehem
was not in finery or show,
but in generosity, humility, purpose and love.
Let us remember – and be glad.
Amen.

Spiritual and physical

God of spirit and imagination,
let our fancies fly
and our spirits soar,
when we hear of good deeds
and see generous hearts at work.
Let us also admire physical feats,
the delights and achievements of sport,
in competition and in teams,
as we remember the team of disciples
who stretched themselves in spreading your word.
Amen.

Lord of the heart,
may our spirits be raised by the knowledge of you.
May our eyes be lifted as we hear your word.
Let our bodies be our temple
as we exercise and contend,
in competition or against the clock.
Let us coordinate mind and body,
spirit and prayer,
in pursuit of your truth.
Amen.

Lord of mind and spirit,
give us a true appreciation of celestial sounds,
in music, in voice, in words, in prayer.
May the gift of silence crowd out the sound of noise.
May we value balance in all things,
rhythm in most things,
and harmony as well as melody.
Amen.

God of vision and purpose,
give us the goal of meeting our potential,
in a world where you have shown
that nothing is impossible with you.
Put us to work to your greater glory.
And along the way may we appreciate
the joys of excellence
in those who have practised and sharpened their skills,
spiritually and physically, to your glory.
Amen.

Lord God,
bringer of music and mystery,
of Olympic talents,
of great works of literature,
of amazing feats of endurance,
let us be inspired to understand you
in the achievements of others;
in the example of friends;
in our own talents,
begun, continued and culminated
in your love for us.
Amen.

The unborn

God of first and last,
protect the unborn,
conceived in love,
deserving of your grace and favour.
Bring them to full life
as a testimony to your faithfulness,
as a test of our responsibility.
As we remember your Son's name,
may we never forget the role of Mary,
our Saviour's safeguard,
from conception to birth,
to death and resurrection.
Amen.

Lord unseen, but known,
have mercy on offspring known but not yet seen,
whether conceived in love or lust.
May they have equal rights to your love;
may they have equal love from those around them;
so that they may grow in confidence,
grow in faith, grow in showing the love to others
that they were shown by your grace,
and by our fond care.
Amen.

God of grace,
you see into our hearts and minds.
You also see before and after in time and space.
We thank you for all the love shown to us
before we came into this world.
And just as you care for us now,
in preparation for the world to come,

DIVERSITY

so may we give special thought and prayer
for the yet unborn;
for the stillborn;
for those who struggle even before birth;
and for those who struggle in infancy.
Amen.

Lord of waiting,
we pray for mothers as they wait to give birth.
Help them to have patience and stamina,
endurance and hope.
Relieve them of too much worry, Lord.
Save them from too much pain,
as nature takes its course,
but with a helping hand to grasp
and a Saviour Christ who understands
the meaning and purpose of waiting,
and the promise of peace after pain.
Amen.

Heavenly Father,
you know the pangs of creation
and importance of rest.
Help mothers and fathers to show
the same love of their creation
that you have shown to us.
May the joys ahead herald a new relationship,
in the same way as the bright star over Bethlehem
heralded a new birth, a new beginning,
in your relationship with humankind.
Amen.

The dead

God of past and present,
may death have no dominion over life.
Bring us to a proper understanding
of the links between,
and the contrasts of,
life and death, presence and absence.
Let fond memories be the bridge
and your love be the link,
always there, but often not perceived.
Open our eyes to the power of the dead
in making our lives fuller,
in giving us hope, even in our grief.
Amen.

Amazing grace, saving Lord,
give us the capacity to remember the dead,
not with sadness but with gratitude,
not with anger but with love,
not with guilt but with joy.
Just as we are born to die,
so we live that we might be with you,
in this life and in eternal life,
as long as we hold our faith and our nerve,
as you have always held us in the palm of your hand.
Amen.

Changing and changeless God,
help us to understand death, not fear it.
In celebrating those who have gone before,
may we see into the mystery you have in store.
We want to see again those we have known,
as well as meet those we never knew.
Give us hope that we can do both.
If it is your will, it will be our delight.
Amen.

Loving Lord,
you know the pain of death,
through the comfort of your Son
and his tears at the death of others.
Bring us your insight and compassion
when we see the effects of death
in ourselves and in others.
Strengthen us to give comfort,
knowing that you are there to hold our hands
and strengthen our hearts.
Amen.

Father of all,
may we set our sights on you when we feel bereft.
You are our first link with the dead,
not a last resort when all else fails.
Give us encouragement that all is well,
faith that we can carry on,
and trust that the souls departed
are safe in your hands,
loving Lord, saving grace.
Amen.

Planning and spontaneity

God of great organisation,
you have brought us untold complexity and richness
alongside great simplicity and beauty.
Yet each new day brings new experiences,
new insights into your creation.
Give our lives form and planning,
alongside spontaneous moments of joy.
Amen.

Lord of life,
thank you for the blessing of planning,
but may we beware of the curse of regimentation.
Let us be good planners of strategy,
but flexible tacticians, responsive beings.
Your Son showed us the importance of questions
rather than giving easy answers.
May we accept the challenge of difficult questions,
by digging deep into your well of wisdom
and keeping close to your purpose in us.
Amen.

God of substance and certainty,
help us in our frailty of purpose
when we are under pressure.
May we always have a plan B
when our organisation fails us.
But let us base our plans on the rock of faith,
so that, like Peter, we may bounce back
and do you proud.
Amen.

Soul-searching Lord,
test us and prove us,
in word and deed, in sorrow and joy,
so that we can truly serve you,
in our planning and your mission.
Help us to hear
as we learn to listen.
Teach us to train
as well as respond
to your love, to others' need,
to your bright flame.
Amen.

Creator, innovator and friend,
may we serve you with our whole mind,
planning, organising, managing, executing.
But may we also serve you with our hearts,
spontaneously, generously, responsively, gladly.
Make us worthy of your extravagant plan
to restore us to you,
through your Son, Jesus Christ.
Amen.

The healthy and the sick

God of health and wholeness,
we ask for your blessings
on all who are hurting at this time,
through physical pain or mental distress.
May their spirits be raised
by what we do and say.
Most of all, Lord, hold out your healing hand,
and give them the promise
of your comforting presence.
Amen.

Lord of restoration and recovery,
let us rejoice in physical and mental health,
the joy of being well,
the blessing of staying healthy.
But let us not forget the struggle of illness,
when food, drink and material things mean little.
May we build up our spiritual resources
so that when illness strikes
we can respond positively to others as to ourselves.
Amen.

Serene Lord,
may we draw on the serenity of your presence
when we experience the confusion of our illness.
May we take heart from the miracles performed by your Son,
and continued through the disciples.
And may the modern-day miracles of treatment and care
go hand in hand with the privilege
of looking after one another,
in his steps and to your glory.
Amen.

Suffering servant, healing Lord,
let us give thanks that where there is illness,
there is often a cure, courtesy of your creation;
and that when a cure is not available,
you give us other strengths and skills
to show our love for each other,
as well as the desire to search,
search, and search again,
for the strands and signs
in your world and in our minds,
which will unlock the answer.
Amen.

Immanent God,
may your presence
teach us patience,
bring us transformation,
point us to the right treatment.
Help our bodies to help themselves;
keep us positive, even in suffering;
and may we always acknowledge
your presence in our ministry to others.
Amen.

Despair and hope

God of consolation,
be with us in our darkest moments,
when all seems lost and we feel alone.
Banish despair from our hearts
and bring hope in its place,
as we rest in your arms.
May we recognise our vulnerability
as we reach out to you,
and you hold us tight.
Amen.

Lord of love,
show your love to the troubled and fragile.
Strengthen them in their tribulations,
mighty Counsellor, true friend.
Let the healing begin
as the causes reveal themselves.
Let the transformation last
through the constancy of prayer.
Surprise us, Lord, by the hope of help
and the promise of what's to come.
Amen.

God of tough love,
create in us, we pray,
a living well of prayerful power,
begun, continued and ended in you.
May every day bring new possibilities
to replace lost options.
May positive relationships
banish the memories of broken ones.
Let love return on the flood tide
to renew and refresh.
Amen.

DIVERSITY

Heavenly Father,
who sees all things, knows all things,
calm the rough seas of our hearts
and quell the turmoil in our minds.
Let calm reign;
let peace rule;
and may we know the certainty
of your sure hope.
Amen.

Father of all,
let the great hopes of youth
be followed by the sure foundations of faith.
And when troubles come,
and everything seems shaky,
let us recall those hopes, those sure foundations,
confident that, whatever life throws at us,
despair is no match for the love you show,
and the love we receive,
through Jesus Christ.
Amen.

Abuse

Sovereign Lord,
we know that love turned bad
can lead to horrible things.
Let our hearts go out to those who have been abused,
and our powers of forgiveness be tested by those who have abused.
We all fall short in our lives.
But let us always call on you,
when feelings of hate or revenge threaten to take over.
Save us from ourselves and bring us back to your true path.
Amen.

Astounding, transforming God,
where you have given us free will
we may stray from the right course.
May we be ever vigilant,
in ourselves and in our dealings with others,
so that evil does not take hold,
damage is not done,
and abuse is confronted.
We pray for victims and perpetrators,
that time and treatment will heal,
with your help, Lord.
Amen.

Maker of heaven and earth,
you have shown us good and warned us of evil.
May we learn the lessons of the past,
in ourselves and over time.
Let us be aware of the signs of abuse,
unafraid of challenging behaviour,
but always seeking remedies
for body and soul, heart and mind,
knowing the extent of your reach.
Amen.

God of transformation,
help those traumatised by abuse
be shown the power of true love,
by neighbour, friend and family,
so that the effects of abuse
can never close the channels to that love,
whatever went before.
Amen.

Loving Lord,
against all odds may untainted, unconditional love prevail,
the love your Son showed us,
the love which restores,
the love which forgives,
the love which respects,
the love which can overcome abuse,
as long as we can trust you
and begin to trust each other again.
Amen.

Alcohol addiction

Almighty God,
you have given us the bread of life,
but also our daily bread.
You have given us living water,
as well as water to drink.
But let us beware the effects of alcohol,
especially when we drink too much too often.
If we are addicted, help us to admit it;
if we seek to recover, make us strong in saying no.
Bless and preserve our will to be free
of harm to self or others.
Amen.

All-embracing Lord,
forgive us our frailties and temptations
as we seek to shed our addictions.
Let the demon drink be overcome
as Satan was resisted in the desert.
But we must remember Satan's
'what though the field be lost, all is not lost'
in keeping up the battle against drink, drugs,
and all that enslaves.
Amen.

All-enveloping Lord,
surround us with hope and trust
in your steely support
as we battle to resist addiction,
in ourselves and in loved ones.
May we be swift to learn
and slow to judge.

Let us be single-minded in our faith
and purposeful in our recovery,
seeking forgiveness for weakness
and showing discipline in rehabilitation.
Amen.

God of remedy and reconciliation,
help the families of those addicted to drink,
in their sensitive situation.
Give them the patience of Job;
give to addicts Peter's ability to learn from failure;
give to friends a constancy that will be tested,
and let the tentacles of drink
release their grip on lives that
once were lost and now are found again.
Amen.

God of fruit and vine,
as we sip our cocktail or swig our beer,
let us pause for thought.
As we quaff our wine
or savour our favourite spirit,
let us reflect.
All things should be in moderation,
except our love for you.
Amen.

Cancer

Healing Lord,
let nature and the skills of doctors
join forces to mend and tend
all afflicted with cancer.
Let diagnosis be quick and treatment timely,
and may the knowledge of your presence
be a comfort and a shield,
to patient and carer alike.
Amen.

God of the personal,
help us never to make assumptions about people's illness
or the treatment they receive.
May every step of recovery from cancer
be blessed with understanding and thanks,
and every setback be accompanied
by renewed prayer and encouragement.
May we combine the cure of disease with the cure of souls.
Amen.

God of great gifts,
send me your love;
show me your concern.
But moderate our expectations,
even as we seek your extravagant generosity.
May we live in hope
and hold on in faith,
until the outcome is known
and your peace takes over.
Amen.

God of purpose and promise,
you take us through the stormy seas of life,
surfing on waves of joy
and plunging into depths of despair.
Be our strong captain
in navigating us through,
and may we ride out the weather,
knowing the calm to come.
Amen.

Lord of healing and wholeness,
we pray for those recovering from cancer
and those whose treatment is just beginning.
As each person is different and distinct,
so each illness is personal and individual.
May we show our empathy,
not only in our words and wishes,
but also in our practical assistance,
those little unremembered acts
of kindness, love and friendship.
Amen.

Coping with suffering

Soothing Lord,
remember us as we cope with pain
and strengthen us in our resolve to recover.
You send us the blessing of life,
but also the trial of tough times.
Thank you for the resilience we have
and the patient friendship of family and friends.
Give us the grace to accept what we experience
alongside the hope of deliverance.
Amen.

All-seeing God,
may we give ourselves to your care,
in partnership with all you have gifted
with medical, nursing and care skills.
May drugs do their work;
may surgeons display their expertise;
and may doctors fulfil their duty of care.
But at the centre of everything,
may we see your bright star,
to ease our pain and see us home.
Amen.

Dear Lord,
heal us,
strengthen us,
prepare us,
care for us.
And whatever surprises we encounter,
hear us,
comfort us,
enfold us,
give us peace.
Amen.

DIVERSITY

Source of light and hope,
give us the strength to cope, in mind and spirit,
with all that life throws at us.
In between the joy and the success,
help us to handle suffering and failure.
May we recognise that we learn more about ourselves
when things go wrong.
Let us respond well and without hesitation
to the suffering of others as well as our own.
Amen.

God of compassion,
create in us, we pray, the capacity to cope,
in illness, in pain, in heartbreak.
Set our spirits free to lift us up
when our body seems to let us down.
Let faith flower in adversity.
Amen.

Crime

God of judgement and forgiveness,
when temptation strikes and people do wrong,
may they soon know the error of their ways
and recognise the hurt they have caused.
And in repaying their debt to society,
may society in turn forgive,
as your Son forgave the criminal on the cross,
so that faith is restored
and restoration can be made.
Amen.

God of justice,
you set us clear standards
and give us ten commandments.
May those who transgress
know the pain of the victims:
and even where there are no obvious victims
may they realise how they have done harm.
So let rehabilitation replace guilt
and restorative justice overcome hate.
Amen.

Almighty God,
you have given us an alternative
to selfishness and crime.
May those who have practised evil ways
see that your way is the better way,
that helping yourself harms others,
that using unreasonable force brings needless hurt.
May our justice mirror your judgement,
slow to chide and swift to forgive,
where repentance is clear
and sorrow is genuine.
Amen.

DIVERSITY

Loving Lord,
may we live by example,
showing mercy and upholding justice.
Create in society
a desire for community.
Give to communities
a will to make things work,
taking responsibility for developing mutual support,
not fomenting sectarian hate.
Amen.

God of grace,
we have all done wrong,
not just in words and action,
but in our thoughts and intentions.
Have pity on those who have gone too far
in giving expression to those evil thoughts
and have paid the penalty.
May they be transformed by the experience,
not to be hardened criminals
but to be restored citizens,
faithful to you and good neighbours to others.
Amen.

Dealing with difficult people

Inclusive Lord,
help us deal with difficult people;
not just those we don't like,
but those who really annoy us.
May we look into our hearts – and theirs,
to understand why they are difficult
and why we find it hard to relate to them.
Give us the patience and the ability
to set a good example,
in faith and trust.
Amen.

God of variety and diversity,
may we always see the good in people,
but beware of the bad,
not in a judgemental way,
but in a developmental one.
Give us the means and the perseverance
to make a stand,
in a gentle way,
to encourage a change,
in an incremental way.
Amen.

God of relationship,
send us a lifeline of harmony,
when relations are strained
and tempers flair.
Give to others and ourselves
a reason to reflect
and time to pause,
so that misunderstandings can be addressed,
differences disentangled from upset,
and peace restored.
Amen.

DIVERSITY

God of stillness,
let silence break out when disputes flair up,
and when we encounter difficulty in others,
let us take deep breaths
before responding in kind;
and then may we show we are listening,
even when we don't quite believe what we hear.
Secure in us, we pray, a readiness to cope,
a desire to reconcile,
as your Son did.
Amen.

Lord of all saints and all souls,
help us to understand the present
through the lessons of the past.
We know now when difficult people
were not challenged or calmed,
when personal vendettas become national disputes,
often leading to wars and destruction.
Help us to avoid escalation of difference,
without compromising confrontation of evil.
Amen.

Debt

Redeeming Lord,
you have forgiven our debts to you,
our transgressions and omissions.
May we be equally forgiving of others
as we seek to be true to your Son,
Jesus Christ.
Amen.

Generous Lord,
keep us as the apple of your eye,
despite our many shortcomings.
Hide us under the shadow of your wings,
even though we let you down.
May we show our hospitality to others,
protection in the storm,
asylum under persecution,
not because they are indebted to us,
but because of our debt to you.
Amen.

God of grace,
bring us the fruits of your Son's sacrifice,
in all that we are and all that we do.
May debts be cancelled,
not just every seven years,
but each time we glimpse your love,
in the acts of kindness of others
and the overwhelming extravagance
of the gift of your Son.
Amen.

DIVERSITY

Loving Lord,
give us the benefit of the doubts we have.
Strengthen our faith in the practice of your grace.
Let the full glory of your gift of creation
always be in our minds,
as we seek to be good stewards of your world,
discharging our great debt to you,
which we can never fully grasp.
Amen.

God of great generosity,
we your unworthy servants
praise and thank you,
in the way we acknowledge our debt to you,
in the way you have removed that debt,
in the way you encourage us to forgive the debts of others.
Let the river of your extravagance
pour down like silver,
an ever-flowing stream of kindness and love.
Amen.

Dementia

Ever-faithful Lord,
forgive our forgetfulness, whenever and wherever it occurs.
And in our old age help us to focus on you,
even when other things are unclear to us.
May the residual memories and knowledge of you
break out of the cloud of unknowing
and set us free.
Amen.

Eternal Father,
your Son taught us the importance of things that last
and the transience of the material world.
In the dementia that afflicts those of all ages,
but especially the elderly,
give hope and flashes of clarity
amidst the fog of forgetfulness.
Let the spirit of your presence
be evident in the hearts of those affected,
even if it is hidden from our sight.
Amen.

Great and glorious God,
let the translucence of your presence
always show through the hesitations and repetitions of dementia.
May our patience and perception
not be found wanting,
as we seek the person within,
and the spirit of faith,
in gesture and twinkle, in touch and gaze,
guided by your bright star.
Amen.

God of spirit and truth,
may the practice of the Eucharist
break through barriers of memory,
as we give thanks through bread and wine.
Let those with all their frailties intact
be especially sensitive to those whose gifts are restricted.
May we always respect the person,
as your Son respected all.
Amen.

Lord of life,
renew in us a right spirit,
towards stranger and sufferer,
as well as neighbour and friend.
We never know when illness will strike,
gradually or all at once.
Let us look out for the needs
and struggles of those with dementia,
not through enlightened self-interest,
but through love of humankind,
love of your creation.
Amen.

Divorce

Lord of unity and diversity,
what you have brought together
may sometimes be put asunder,
given our fallen state.
We ask your forgiveness and patience,
long-suffering Lord.
We ask for the second chance
that you gave to humankind,
through your Son.
Amen.

God of justice and mercy,
look down on the imperfection of humankind,
breathe a sigh, shed a tear,
and help us to face up to divorce,
if that is the only way forward.
May repentance and forgiveness
be the right way to part
and the only way to move on.
Amen.

Lord God,
you brought man and woman together to care for each other
and to bring forth children, if that is your will.
Let delight in companionship
and the responsibility of parenthood
bring joy, not strife.
But if it proves to be not of you
that these two people should remain together,
may the parting of the ways
be as clear as the parting of the waves,
and may both parties pass through unscathed.
Amen.

God of peace and reconciliation,
even if divorce is inevitable,
let there be peace in the process
and reconciliation of difference and diversity,
as separation and the parting of the ways
bring such sweet sorrow
and resignation to being apart.
Sorry, Lord, for what we have done
and for what we have left undone.
Amen.

Lord of love,
we have let you down
when a marriage crumbles.
Help us to shoulder blame and responsibility,
if we have contributed
to the pressure and pain of separation.
But let us also take the responsibility
of mending lives,
through prayer, through listening,
through being there for people,
in the hope of reconciliation,
in the expectation of a second chance.
Amen.

Domestic violence

God of peace,
we lift up to you
all those who are victims of domestic violence,
who suffer in silence
and simmer in resentment.
May they have the courage to resist assertively
and report or raise the alarm.
May bullies never prosper
where you are Lord of all.
Amen.

Saviour God, Prince of peace,
may we always be aware
of the early warnings of domestic violence,
in ourselves and in those we love.
Help us to head off growing resentment
and ensure that differences are talked through
without resort to raised voices or raised hands.
May the sun never set
without a resolution of resentments.
And let the power of prayer and contemplation
always be preferable to instant reaction,
done or said in anger.
Help us to respect and forgive in an atmosphere of calm,
just as we pray to you in the midst of turmoil.
Amen.

God of our fathers,
send us the hope of reconciliation
after the despair of aggression.
Let domestic dispute lead to domestic understanding,
without the oppression of the cycle of destruction,
which can turn reason to unreason,

sweetness to bitterness,
discussion to violence.
Cast out violence from our nature,
transforming Lord.
Amen.

God of first and last,
may reason be first and violence be last
in our repertoire of response.
Let self-defence prevent the worst
and may assertiveness and the art of listening
calm emotion and avoid escalation.
Amen.

Transforming Lord,
send us out in sympathy
for those who experience domestic violence.
Send us out in confidence
to cope with perpetrators of violence.
Safeguard us from danger,
but let us not shrink
from saying things which challenge unacceptable behaviour,
knowing that your Son upset the tables of the money-changers,
but did not countenance violence to person,
except when he accepted humankind's violence to him.
Amen.

Drugs

God of steadfast love,
save us from the diversion of drugs,
the insidious craving and the dependence.
Let us be alert to the symptoms,
in ourselves and in others,
of a reliance on substances
which cause addiction and damage.
Thank you, Lord.

Lord of all,
let us delight in trying new tastes,
in sampling the fruits of your creation.
But keep us from depending on anything or anyone,
except you, as our plumb-line and lodestar,
an ever-present help in trouble,
and the source of all true joy.
Amen.

Saviour, Servant, Sovereign,
all things come from you,
but you have given us the free will
to consume too much
and to fail to respect our bodies and our minds,
so dishonouring you.
Keep our hearts, minds and bodies
free from false gods, evil cravings,
and, even when we fail,
bring us back to you, we pray.
Amen.

Father of all,
when we stray, pull us back;
when we are on the edge, do not allow us to tip over;
when we feel at the end of our tether,
help us to realise that you are there at the other end,
if we just acknowledge you
and depend on no other.
Amen.

Lord God,
set us free from drugs in all their forms.
Help us to recognise, in ourselves and others around us,
the tell-tale signs of absenteeism and introspection.
May those who battle with addiction
and those who confront the drug pushers and smugglers
have success as well as support
in their difficult tasks.
Amen.

Family breakdown

God of family and friendship,
may all that occurs in families
be blessed with an openness of spirit
and a wave of unconditional love.
Let us be open to challenges,
but always enfolded in the love which binds us,
and the love you have shown to us,
through your Son, Jesus Christ.
Amen.

Astonishing Lord,
who made heaven and earth,
and brought man and woman into the world,
to your delight and our eternal gratitude,
let us be worthy of your trust
and the second chance you have given us,
to give firm foundations to family members
and true friendship to neighbours,
as your Son taught us.
Amen.

Long-suffering Lord,
bring us patience and perseverance
in maintaining family relationships,
turning disunity into harmony,
jealousy or envy into trust.
May we set an example to the next generation
by promoting your values
and worshipping your holy name,
through Jesus Christ.
Amen.

Amazing God,
you sent your Son as a member of the human family,
to have and to hold,
to worship and adore.
Let us model your generosity
in all our family dealings,
as the father of the prodigal son showed us
and the mother of your Son proved to us.
Amen.

Lord of relationship,
make families secure;
may each generation be grateful to the last;
may family feuds turn into family friendships;
may our hearts be gladdened at family achievements,
but, above all:
let us know your blessings,
in our homes, in our households,
and in our family celebrations,
Father God.
Amen.

Gambling

Sure and certain Lord,
let us take risks for you,
but not gambles for us.
Chance is a fine thing
but an unworthy master.
Keep us from relying on the toss of a coin
or a roll of the dice,
and keep us focused on you.
Amen.

Lord of winning and losing,
teach us to cope with setbacks
and to survive successes,
but don't let us, for one moment,
believe that winning by chance
is the key to happiness
or that losing a lottery
is the end of the world.
Keep us on an even keel, Lord.
Thank you.
Amen.

Universal Lord,
as we survey the orderliness of your creation
we know that it wasn't accidental,
a galactic gamble that failed.
This was, and is, a marvel of imagination,
a leap of faith in us
which we can only respond to
in admiration and wonder.
Amen.

Ingenious, spontaneous God,
we ask you to moderate our restless nature
when we bet too much on worthless things,
as if we can't believe our luck.
Help us to understand,
without the risk of gambling,
that we can experience a real buzz
just adoring you and enjoying your great works.
Amen.

Great God of power and passion,
save gamblers from ruining lives,
their own and the lives of the ones they love.
May they hold back on risking all
in games of chance against all odds,
but in their risks
may they understand the extent
of the greatest risk of all,
taken by your Son to save us
and restore our relationship with you.
Amen.

Politics

Lord of hearts and minds,
send down on politicians
the gift of wisdom and the humility of servants.
May they learn to challenge the status quo
but never to change for change's sake.
Teach them to hear as well as listen
and act at all times with integrity,
as your Son taught us.
Amen.

Sovereign Lord,
there is always a tide in the affairs of humankind,
which takes us on or sets us back.
Help all who govern discern the pattern of that tide
and know how to ride the surf
and avoid the quicksand.
Amen.

Lord of strategy and oversight,
assist those who seek election
and stay with them if they take power.
May they set their sights high
but keep their feet on the ground.
Guide them, encourage them,
but let them understand
when it is time to go.
Amen.

Almighty God,
you showed us through your Son
that the art of politics
is not to confront or control,
but to question and reflect back,
to lead by example,
not to misuse power.
Grant our politicians the vision
to make a difference to people's lives
without thought for their own.
Amen.

Heavenly Father,
look down on our different forms of democracy
with benign and generous oversight.
May we understand the sheer diversity of mechanisms
to ensure the election and maintenance
of a proper government
and a means for voting them out.
May there always be a way of rendering to Caesar what is Caesar's,
and to God what is God's.
Amen.

War and peace

God of peace,
may we so hate war
that we go the extra mile for peace.
May the threat or rumour of war
concentrate the minds of politicians and armies
to pull back from confrontation
and give reconciliation a chance.
Amen.

Lord of integrity and purpose,
may we stop war in its tracks
by honouring diversity,
not by forcing uniformity.
You made us all different,
so let us celebrate that difference.
May peace be the natural order,
not one imposed by force.
May we know that through your Son,
Jesus Christ.
Amen.

Father God,
who makes all things new,
let peace break out in unlikely places,
by dint of brave words and courageous acts.
You have shown us over time
that miracles happen,
especially in the people and places
we least expect.
Surprise us, Lord.
Amen.

God of transformation,
peace you gave to us,
peace you expect of us.
Commission us to banish war
by sharing peace,
by sharing you, in bread and wine,
in church and society.
Amen.

Rewarding Lord,
let us not look to heaven to heal all ills,
when your kingdom extends to earth
and we have a job to do here.
May we follow you to the ends of the earth,
not to dominate or dictate,
but to be good stewards
of your world, your peace,
your answer to the dead end of unjust wars.
Amen.

Other **Rupert Bristow** books

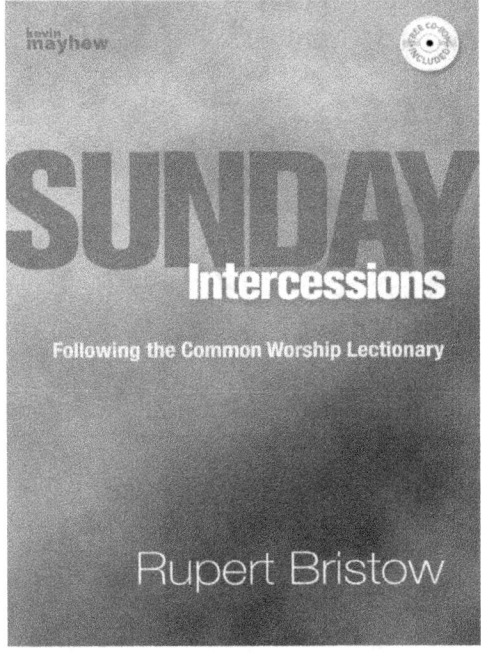

Sunday Intercessions
Paperback 1501222
Hardback 1501326

www.kevinmayhew.com

Prayers for Parishes
1501256

www.kevinmayhew.com

Only Connect
1501167

www.kevinmayhew.com

www.ingramcontent.com/pod-product-compliance
Lightning Source LLC
Chambersburg PA
CBHW051352070526
44584CB00025B/3735